Cambridge Discovery Education

▶ **INTERACTIVE**

Series editor: Bob H

CROCS AND GATORS

A1

Simon Beaver

CAMBRIDGE
UNIVERSITY PRESS

Discovery
EDUCATION

CAMBRIDGE
UNIVERSITY PRESS

University Printing House, Cambridge CB2 8BS, United Kingdom

One Liberty Plaza, 20th Floor, New York, NY 10006, USA

477 Williamstown Road, Port Melbourne, VIC 3207, Australia

314–321, 3rd Floor, Plot 3, Splendor Forum, Jasola District Centre, New Delhi – 110025, India

103 Penang Road, #05-06/07, Visioncrest Commercial, Singapore 238467

Cambridge University Press is part of the University of Cambridge.

It furthers the University's mission by disseminating knowledge in the pursuit of education, learning and research at the highest international levels of excellence.

www.cambridge.org
Information on this title: www.cambridge.org/9781107655072

First published 2014

20 19 18 17 16 15 14 13 12 11 10 9

Printed in Great Britain by CPI Group (UK) Ltd, Croydon CR0 4YY

A catalogue record for this publication is available from the British Library.

Library of Congress Cataloguing in Publication data
Beaver, Simon.
 Crocs & gators / Simon Beaver.
  pages cm. -- (Cambridge discovery interactive readers)
 ISBN 978-1-107-65507-2 (pbk. : alk. paper)
1. Crocodiles--Juvenile literature. 2. Alligators--Juvenile literature. 3. English language--Textbooks for foreign speakers. 4. Readers (Elementary) I. Title. II. Title: Crocs and gators.
QL666.C925B42 2013
597.98'2--dc23

2013024134

ISBN 978-1-107-65507-2

Additional resources for this publication at www.cambridge.org

Cambridge University Press has no responsibility for the persistence or accuracy of URLs for external or third-party internet websites referred to in this publication, and does not guarantee that any content on such websites is, or will remain, accurate or appropriate.

Layout services, art direction, book design, and photo research: Q2ABillSMITH GROUP
Editorial services: Hyphen S.A.
Audio production: CityVox, New York
Video production: Q2ABillSMITH GROUP

Contents

Before You Read: Get Ready!

Crocodiles and alligators are very interesting animals. How much do you really know about them?

A crocodile　　　　　　　　An alligator

Words to Know

Look at the pictures. Then complete the sentences with the correct words.

jaws　　　　　　the wild　　　　　　skin

1 You can see crocodiles in zoos and also in _____.

2 That crocodile has a lot of teeth in its strong _____.

3 You can make bags or shoes from the _____ of alligators and crocodiles.

4

Words to Know

Read the paragraph. Then complete the sentences with the correct highlighted words.

When animals can have babies together, we say they are a species. Some species, like crocodiles and alligators, are dangerous. These reptiles are safe when they are small babies, but then they grow bigger. When they become adults, they also become very dangerous.

1 Indira is studying to _____ a doctor.

2 Sequoia trees _____ to 100 meters tall.

3 Dogs are a _____ . Any kinds of dogs can have babies together.

4 Crocodiles and alligators are _____ .

5 Don't drive so fast. It's _____ !

Comparatives

Look at the animals. Choose the right words in the sentences below.

A long snake

A small lizard

A big crocodile

1 The crocodile is bigger / smaller than the lizard.

2 The snake is longer / shorter than the lizard.

3 The lizard is fatter / thinner than the crocodile.

4 The crocodile is more dangerous / less dangerous than the lizard.

5 The crocodile is the biggest / smallest reptile.

5

CHAPTER 1

Alligators and Crocodiles: True or False?

THERE ARE A LOT OF STORIES ABOUT THESE ANIMALS. WHICH ARE TRUE?

❶ *Crocodiles cry.* People often say that crocodiles (or crocs) cry. Is that right?

❷ *Alligators live under the streets of New York.* There is a story that there are a lot of very big alligators (or gators) in the sewers[1] under the streets of New York. True?

❸ *Alligators are only fast in the water.* Many people think that alligators are slow when they aren't swimming. Are they?

❹ *You can easily stop a crocodile from opening its jaws.* Can a person do that?

....

[1]**sewers:** the places under a city where dirty water goes

1. True. Crocodiles cry, but not because they're unhappy. Water comes from their eyes when they eat!

2. False. Gators need the sun. It's too dark in sewers. And too cold in the winter.

3. False. Alligators can run at 17 **kilometers** an hour! But only for a short time.

4. True. A crocodile's jaws are very strong when it closes them but not when it opens them. So, it cannot open its mouth if you put your hands around its jaws. But you have to be very **careful**! Crocs are dangerous!

CHAPTER 2

All About Crocodiles

HOW MUCH DO YOU KNOW ABOUT CROCODILES?

Crocodilians (crocodiles and alligators) are reptiles. Reptiles are animals that come from eggs, like birds. Reptiles are cold-**blooded** animals – they need the sun to stay warm. Because they don't use food to make their body warm, they don't need to eat much.

It's easy to see if a crocodilian is an alligator or a crocodile. Their heads aren't the same. The alligator's head looks like a U from above. The crocodile's head is longer and thinner and looks like a V.

An alligator

A crocodile

The first crocodiles lived more than 20 million years ago. Today, they live all around the world: in Africa, the Americas, Asia, and Australia. Some live in rivers and others live in the sea.

Crocodiles can swim fast: 32 kilometers an hour! And they can stay underwater for more than an hour!

There are different species of crocodile. Some **grow** very big and some are smaller. The smallest adults are under two **meters** long. But the biggest croc of all time was 6.2 meters!

? ANALYZE
Birds also come from eggs. How are they different from reptiles?

9

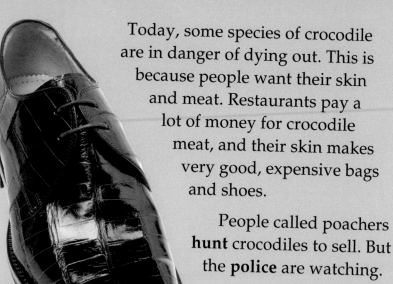

Today, some species of crocodile are in danger of dying out. This is because people want their skin and meat. Restaurants pay a lot of money for crocodile meat, and their skin makes very good, expensive bags and shoes.

People called poachers **hunt** crocodiles to sell. But the **police** are watching.

All the countries in the world say that you mustn't hunt one species: the Siamese crocodile. In 2012, police in China caught poachers with 3,600 Siamese crocodiles! They think that restaurants in Guangdong wanted to buy the crocodiles for their meat. The police took the crocs back to the wild.

Crocodile skin

Crocodiles don't like other animals to come near them.

In a zoo in Australia, a crocodile called Elvis thought a new lawnmower was another animal. The lawnmower made a lot of noise when the men at the zoo used it. Elvis jumped on it and carried it into the water! He stayed with it for more than an hour. The men couldn't get it back.

Later, when the men got the lawnmower, they found two of Elvis's teeth in it. Lawnmowers aren't good to eat! The zoo had to buy a new lawnmower.

Video Quest

Saltwater Crocodiles

Watch the video about saltwater crocodiles and freshwater crocs. How are they different?

CHAPTER 3

See You Later, Alligator

WHEN PEOPLE LEAVE, THEY SOMETIMES SAY "SEE YOU LATER, ALLIGATOR." BUT WHAT IS AN ALLIGATOR?

Crocodiles and alligators **became** different families[2] of animals about 37 million years ago. Crocodiles live in many countries, but we usually only find alligators in the United States and China.

We know that crocodiles and alligators have different heads. But their color is different, too. Crocodiles are usually gray-green. Alligators are usually dark brown or black.

Big adult alligators are about four meters long. People think the biggest alligator grew to 5.85 meters! It lived in Louisiana, USA.

[2]**family:** a group of species that aren't very different

American alligators eat a lot of fish. But they also eat small animals, other reptiles – and other alligators! They need good teeth. Alligators grow new teeth all the time. One alligator can have 3,000 teeth in its life!

Male alligators "dance" to find **females** and have babies. At night, a lot of alligators meet and "dance" together.

The females have 20–50 eggs at one time. But not all of these eggs become adult alligators.

EVALUATE
Why do you think not all the alligator eggs become adults?

In the wild, alligators can live 30–50 years. But they can live for 70 years in zoos because they have good food and vets.[3] Belgrade Zoo in Serbia has a 76-year-old gator called Mujo. He's maybe the oldest in the world.

In the United States, there are a lot of alligator farms. People go to these farms to buy meat and skin. Like crocodile skin, alligator skin makes good bags and shoes. People also pay to see the alligators in these farms. They're interesting animals.

Alligators aren't good pets. They never learn to love people like cats or dogs do. And adult gators can be very dangerous. In many countries you can't have a pet alligator at home.

[3]**vet:** short for veterinarian, a doctor for animals

In Missouri, USA, different people bought 50 baby alligators from a man called Ken Henderson in 2011. They were very small. But then they grew! Police had to find these "pets" and take them. One woman had two gators in her backyard. Small children lived near her. It wasn't safe!

Video Quest

Alligator Eggs

Watch the video. Why does Jeff Corwin want to find alligator eggs?

CHAPTER 4

People, Crocs, and Gators

CAN WE LIVE WITH CROCS AND GATORS? AND CAN THEY LIVE WITH US?

Are people bad for crocodilians? Yes and no.

We build houses and factories in the places where they live. Pollution from our cars and factories is bad for crocodilians. We eat their meat and make bags with their skin.

There were a lot more crocs and gators in the world 100–200 years ago. Today, there aren't any crocodilians in a lot of places because of people and the things that we do.

There's another problem: the weather around the world is getting warmer. So, there's more rain in some places. And floods. Crocodilians like water, but too much water is bad for their eggs.

What's the answer? In many countries, people make **reserves** or national parks. A reserve is a safe place for animals to live in the wild. There are no houses or factories on reserves. They're clean and there are workers there to help the animals. People can't catch or eat the animals on reserves. More baby crocodilians can live to become adults.

? UNDERSTAND
Why are reserves good for crocodilians?

A flood

Maybe you think that nuclear plants are bad for animals. But the Turkey Point nuclear plant in Florida, USA, is helping crocodilians.

The United States is the only country in the world with both crocodiles and alligators. But 40 years ago, there were only 300 crocodiles in Florida. Today, people think there are between 500 and 2,000.

Many live near Turkey Point. Why? It's because there are little rivers of warm water that come out from the nuclear plant. They are a great place for crocodiles to stay and have babies. So there are more and more crocodiles in Turkey Point.

A nuclear plant

People eat crocodile and alligator meat all around the world. Very often, it comes from farms. The farms need a lot of crocodilians to make money. So there are more crocs and gators because people eat them.

Crocodilians aren't dangerous on farms. But there's a problem for people who live near crocodilians in the wild. Crocs and gators go where they want. They don't always stay out of people's homes. Sometimes, they get into people's backyards and swimming pools. That can be a big problem!

Video Quest

Get the Gator!

Watch the video. Why do Jeff and Todd have to catch the alligator?

CHAPTER 5

What Do You Think?

HOW DO YOU FEEL ABOUT CROCS AND GATORS?

Do you know the story *Peter Pan*? A crocodile eats a clock. The clock stays in its body and makes a noise: tick, tick, tick. The crocodile wants to eat a man called Captain Hook. When Hook hears the noise, he knows the crocodile is near. He runs away. He really doesn't like crocodiles!

Different people have problems with different animals. Which animals do you really not like? Spiders? Snakes? Or are you OK with all animals?

A spider

Did you see a real crocodile or alligator? Where? If not, do you want to see one? Why?

Are there crocodilians in the wild in your country? Can you have one in your home? What other reptile pets do a lot of people have? Do you want a reptile pet?

Did you ever eat crocodile or alligator meat? Where? If not, do you want to eat it? Why? Do you think it's good or bad that people eat crocs and gators? Or can it sometimes be good and sometimes bad? Why?

After You Read

Choose Ⓐ (True) or Ⓑ (False). If the book doesn't tell you, choose Ⓒ (Doesn't say).

1 Crocodiles cry like people.
    Ⓐ True
    Ⓑ False
    Ⓒ Doesn't say

2 Crocodiles have longer, thinner heads than alligators.
    Ⓐ True
    Ⓑ False
    Ⓒ Doesn't say

3 You mustn't hunt Siamese crocodiles.
    Ⓐ True
    Ⓑ False
    Ⓒ Doesn't say

4 Elvis the crocodile was 76 years old.
    Ⓐ True
    Ⓑ False
    Ⓒ Doesn't say

5 Crocodiles and alligators became different families of animals 55 million years ago.
    Ⓐ True
    Ⓑ False
    Ⓒ Doesn't say

6 There are alligators in Africa.
    Ⓐ True
    Ⓑ False
    Ⓒ Doesn't say

7 An alligator can have 3,000 teeth in its life.

- Ⓐ True
- Ⓑ False
- Ⓒ Doesn't say

8 Floods are good for crocodilians.

- Ⓐ True
- Ⓑ False
- Ⓒ Doesn't say

Complete the Text

Use the words in the box to complete the paragraph.

blood	dangerous	reptiles	scales

Snakes, crocodiles, and alligators are all **1** _____.
They have **2** _____ on their skin, and their
3 _____ is cold. Be careful. Crocodilians and snakes
can be **4** _____!

Reptiles and Me

Write down three reptiles you saw. Where did you see them? What did you think about them?

Reptile	Where I saw it	What I thought about it
1.		
2.		
3.		

Answer Key

Words to Know, page 4
1 the wild **2** jaws **3** skin

Words to Know, page 5
1 become **2** grow **3** species **4** reptiles **5** dangerous

Comparatives, page 5
1 bigger **2** longer **3** thinner **4** more dangerous
5 biggest

Understand, page 7
It is too cold and dark in the sewers.

Analyze, page 9
Birds have feathers and wings. Most can fly.

Video Quest, page 11
Saltwater crocodiles are the biggest reptiles in the world.

Evaluate, page 13
Possible answer: Other animals eat the little alligators.

Video Quest, page 15
He wants to take them to a safe place.

Understand, page 17
Crocodilians are safe on reserves. There's no pollution, houses, roads, or factories. People can't hunt them.

Video Quest, page 19
The family can't swim in their pool with an alligator in it.

True or False?, page 22
1 B **2** A **3** A **4** C **5** B **6** B **7** A **8** B

Complete the Text, page 23
1 reptiles **2** scales **3** blood **4** dangerous